Quainton Road Station

and other stations in the

Vale of Aylesbury

BILL SIMPSON

Lamplight Publications

Published by
Lamplight Publications
260 Colwell Drive
Witney
Oxfordshire OX28 5LW

First Published 2011

ISBN: 978 1 899246 52 6

Printed and bound by Information Press
Southfield Road, Eynsham, Oxford OX29 4JB

Contents

Acknowledgements

The author would like to convey thanks to all the following that have contributed to this history. Lance Adlam, David Bent, Anthea Hanscomb, Andrew Bratton, Tim Stevens, Denis J McCulloch, Roy Miller, Rob Riley, Christopher Tayler. Apart from those listed many others have contributed in lesser ways far too numerous to list but nevertheless essential to the result. Collectively they would be regarded as the Quainton Railway Society.

Cover photographs and painting: Bill Simpson
Front cover top: Quainton Road Station
Front cover bottom: Verney Junction Station
Back cover: Quainton Road Station

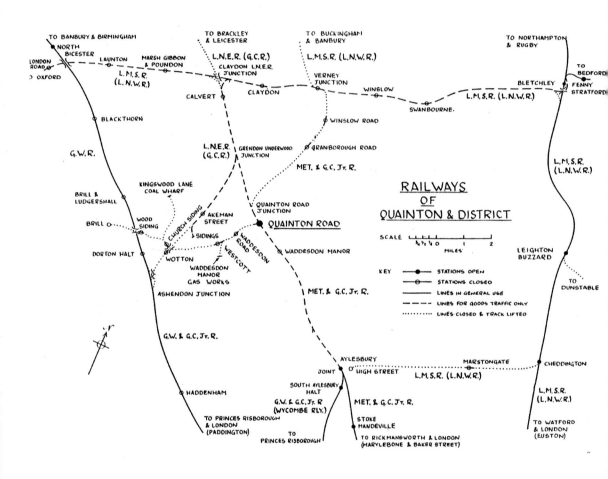

This would be railway access in the Quainton district from 1910-1935.

The original station building built by the Aylesbury & Buckingham Railway immediately north of the road crossing that was replaced by the present road bridge. Note that the station sign just visible under the eve's displays 'Quainton Road' which proves that this was the original name.

The Country Station

Railway stations have from their beginnings provided the essential background to the writers of fiction and there is a very good reason for this. Their purpose provides scenes of real life drama, emotional farewells and reunions at the crucial point where these feelings have a climax. Nowadays some of this role has been taken over by airports, but they can never provide the atmospheric scenario of white palls of steam and reflecting firelight in portmanteau thrillers like Sherlock Holmes.

Whatever the mood of the drama, be it glorious farce like Will Hay at 'Buggleskelly' in 'Oh Mr Porter' or the lovelorn pathos provided by the eternal 'Brief Encounter', it is an aura that exists at all railways, stations big or small.

In the case of Quainton Road station we can only imagine and guess at what scenes have been lived through in front of its old bricks. Originally, a not very successful country railway which had few trains, mostly silence but for the sounds of the countryside. When the Brill Tramway line to Wotton and Brill was opened there would be shouts from men in the 'down' yard north of the village road where they shovelled coal from wagons on the Aylesbury & Buckingham Railway into the lighter wagons used on the tramway to be delivered to Wotton House along with the other requirements for a large house.

Materials moving on the Brill Tramway in the other direction would be bricks and roof tiles produced at the workings around Brill and timber from the Wotton estate, with a contribution from the daily routine of milk churns gathering throughout Buckinghamshire full of milk, then clanking empty homeward for the next days filling.

The 'up' 'Master Cutler' Sheffield - Marylebone passing through Aylesbury in the 1950's. The train would have passed through Quainton Road. In this view it is hauled by an A3 Pacific no 60102 *Sir Frederick Banbury*. This train was transferred to Kings Cross in the mid 1950's whence it ran via Retford until 1958 when it ceased.

G.C. Farnell

The branch also found a role in carrying material to the foot of Lodge Hill to be hoisted up to the construction of Waddesdon Manor that was completed in 1889. A station for the house was opened on the main line south of Quainton on January 1, 1897 on the newly opened Great Central Railway. This was the London extension of the former Manchester, Sheffield & Lincolnshire Railway.

This very localised focus of the railway was to drastically change with the fortunes of the advancing Metropolitan Railway that came over the horizon from London in 1894 and took over this remote junction.

The Great Central Railway brought the sparkle of dining car expresses passing through with a proud shining engine at the head. The Metropolitan also began a service with Pullman cars.

This was dimmed by the effect of two world wars. The first when hundreds of nervous young men assembled on many stations feeling awkward in chaffing new battledress. Men that had never known much beyond the confines of local villages suddenly faced the horrors of trench warfare in a foreign land.

The second war brought the distant glow of the London sky as the city suffered under a rain of fire from would be invaders. During this period Quainton was very busy, apart from trains of war ordnance it also became a depot for the storage of severely rationed foodstocks. The grounds of nearby Waddesdon Manor were used for the storage of jerry cans full of petrol. These were unloaded at Quainton Road station.

After the war there was what now seems like a brief elysian period to discover the joys of train spotting on a railway system that seemed to bask in the glow of restored contentment. It was of course an illusion. Those long summer days that needed so little apart from Ian Allan loco spotters books, sandwiches and lemonade were to be

A map of the area of the line from Aylesbury showing how instead of taking a direct route to the Oxford - Bletchley line through Pichcott Gap it diverted to the west to allow the Duke of Buckingham to connect with his tramway.

shattered beyond recall. In the 1960's most dreams were taken away when lines closed and steam locomotives were scrapped.

Quainton was included on this sad list of unwanted stations and may have been consigned to oblivion, like its neighbouring stations of Waddesdon Manor, Winslow Road and Grandborough Road. However the determination of those that did not want to see the values of another age completely obliterated from our heritage began to assemble. What happened then is further described in subsequent pages of this book.

The history of the railway line upon which Quainton Road station is situated has been chronicled in detail in a number of volumes so it is sufficient to say here that its belated opening took place on September 23, 1868 as a station on the Aylesbury & Buckingham Railway, although the latter place could only be reached by changing trains at Verney Junction north of Quainton. The company that owned the line at

A very interesting aerial view of the station taken after being secured by the QRS. Clearly the early road direct to the village can be seen replaced by the bridge. The buildings on the bottom right are those of the war time food storage depot of the Ministry of Agriculture, Fisheries and Food. The two circulating road areas east and west of the station were built during the war under the Emergency Powers Act to facilitate bi-directional traffic entering the goods yard and food storage depot. The area of land to the north of the bridge (left) was the site of the original Quainton Road station.

Quainton Railway Society Collection

A tank engine of the Great Central Railway, class 12AT converted to a motor working 12AM. It is seen here at Aylesbury early in the twentieth century operating motor working from Aylesbury to Verney Junction through Quainton. This working was the result of the Joint partnership of the Met & GCR Joint whereby the Metropolitan continued with all the through trains between Verney junction and Baker Street

QRS Collection

Quainton shortly after the building of the new station in 1894. The roadbridge followed closely on this work, which has become quickly soot-stained emphasising the intensive use of the line. Note the distant steps giving access to the road avoiding the station driveway. Although the three arch bridge took no other rails it would probably have been built to an existing pattern allowing for any future expanded works at the station as there was existing land purchased by the railway south of the bridge. Note the Metropolitan signals beyond the foot bridge.

Leicestershire County Council

A smart looking rake of former Metropolitan coaches at Aylesbury in the late 1930's.

QRS Collection

The very remarkable view looking north at Quainton after the building of the new station in 1895-6. The Metropolitan have not yet built the new road bridge over the line (1898) so the original road crossing of the A&BR is still in situ. The photograph must have been taken just after the doubling of the track which took place in 1897. The roof of the crossing hut containing signalling instruments can be seen at the far end of the platform. This arrangement remained at the stations on the line to Verney Junction. The crossing at Quainton was closed and removed in 1899.

Leicestershire County Council

Verney Junction to Buckingham, the LNWR , were not kindly disposed to this upstart railway, in fact they asserted that it was economically pointless which they sought to confirm by not timing trains to ease passenger movement between the county towns.

It was a view they had to some degree modify when a company with more muscle power, the Metropolitan Railway, took over the tottering A&BR in July 1890. Consequently new station buildings were erected at Verney Junction and the other stations on the line including Quainton Road. From that time on all things changed dramatically. The Manchester, Sheffield & Lincolnshire Railway began to run coal trains over their new extension in 1898. Passenger trains followed in 1899 by which time the MS&LR became known as the aforementioned Great Central Railway joining with the Metropolitan Railway to form the Metropolitan & Great Central Joint Committee to manage the line for joint usage in 1906 from Quainton Road to Harrow.

When the Great Central joined the Metropolitan Railway some three quarters of a mile north of the station the Metropolitan insisted that the newcomer joined their railway and not the other way round. The result was the severe bend in the fast running track was the cause of a potentially serious accident soon after the opening of the latter. The Board of Trade responsible for the safety of railways insisted that the junction was relaid to suit the fast running of the GCR. The points of this junction became the first in the country to be electrically operated.

During the period of the Aylesbury & Buckingham Railway Quainton Road became a junction for the railway to Brill; this is described further in a subsequent chapter.

When the Metropolitan progressed north of the city with its electrification in 1901 it reached Harrow in 1910 and Rickmansworth in 1925. After reaching Harrow it decided to celebrate electrification with Pullman coaches in certain trains that changed to steam haulage at Harrow. They began to be included in trains from June 1, 1910, with the proclamation that they were the first electrically hauled Pullmans in Europe. Prior to the first World War they were included in trains to Verney Junction and as they ran onto the Circle and Widened Lines right into the city they provided a brief but remarkable service, especially as they also catered for Saturday theatre goers.

Much was to change with the outbreak of war and the return of this service after the war was operated to Aylesbury only. It ceased altogether with the outbreak of the second world war.

However, the transport needs of the capital were becoming hopelessly chaotic with so many separate undertakings of transport and so it was decided that a London Passenger Transport Board should be formed from 1933. This absorbed the Metropolitan Railway becoming integrated under the aegis of London Transport. The new body continued electrification after the second World War to reach Amersham in 1960, but no further.

From Aylesbury to Verney Junction
by Denis J McCulloch

Denis McCulloch is a gentleman that came to Quainton and provided the following account which is a unique first hand experience of the final days of local railways in 1936.

Of the service six of the trips were local between Aylesbury, Quainton Road and Verney Junction only. Generally worked by an ex GER 2-4-2 tank engine with a single ex GCR open composite coach. The last but two and last trips each way were through trains to and from Baker Street and were made up of three or four standard Metropolitan coaches pulled by a 4-4-4 tank or 0-6-4 tank. Quite frequently when one of the 'down' through trains arrived at Verney Junction, the engine worked back to either Winslow Road or Granborough Road collecting what cattle traffic there was then returned it to Verney Junction ready to be sent to London on one of the 'up' through trains. Although first class accommodation was provided on all trains no first class tickets were ever issued from any of the stations.

Waddesdon and Quainton had thirteen trains each way on weekdays, including one 'up' Pullman car service in the morning, and about five trains on Sundays.

The Sunday train service between Quainton Road and Verney Junction was withdrawn in June 1931. This included a reduction of the train service at Quainton Road to six trains each way on weekdays with two 'down' and three 'up' on Sundays.

North of Aylesbury goods have by far been the most important part of the traffic and the goods train service is being maintained between London, Aylesbury, Quainton Road and Verney Junction (to Claydon Junction the line remains in goods service still), but the intermediate stations have been closed to it.

Prior to July 6 Waddesdon received one goods train each way on weekdays only. Quainton Road continues to receive its large total of seven trains each way on weekdays. This includes two LNER trains each way to and from Woodford and Hinton. The number of goods trains at this station is greater than the number of passenger trains. The service between Quainton Road and Verney Junction consists of three trains each way, one of which used to call at Granborough Road and Winslow Road. These trains proceed from Verney Junction to Bletchley and then on to the Northampton District, worked of course by an LMS engine. In addition to these trains there is the LNER milk train to Marylebone on Sunday Mornings and another local milk train on weekdays.

In 1949

On Sunday May 8 1949 I paid a visit to Waddesdon and Quainton to arrange accommodation for the Whitsun weekend. After making enquiries it was decided to stay at The Bell Hotel, Aylesbury.

A journey to Quainton Road station was made by bus. The layout of the station and sidings was unchanged and it was noticeable what large siding accommodation there was, especially on the 'up' side of the line.

The Brill platform and sidings were unchanged except that a Ministry of Food depot had been built nearby. The Brill branch itself was in position for about 200 yards out of the station and served as a siding for the Depot. The site of the first level crossing was completely bare and the hedges cleared away.

At Quainton Road Junction it was noticed that the down line of the Verney Line had been removed.[1]

On Whitsun Weekend the following June on Saturday June 4, we went to Brill from Aylesbury by bus passing the location of stations Waddesdon Road, Westcott, Wotton, Wood Siding (that was still so named on bus timetables) and so to Brill village. We walked down to the site of Brill station.

The yard gate was in position and the fence shown in photographs of 1938 but was rather overgrown. The position of some of the former buildings were still traceable.

We walked along the cutting towards Wood Siding but the way was blocked by bushes. The brickworks appeared disused but the site of the siding was traceable. Inside the brickworks large heaps of sand had been dumped where the siding once was. Rushebeds Wood was largely cut down and the scenery spoilt.

At Wood Siding the gates shown in the 1938 photographs were removed. The site of the station was in a very muddy state and completely spoiled.

We walked along the road to Wotton and inspected the site of Wotton station. The tree trunks shown in the 1938 photographs on the site of the station were still there.

From Wotton station towards Westcott the site of the railway had been turned into a concrete road leading to the RAE RP Depot. We returned by bus from Wotton to Aylesbury.

On Sunday 5 I bought two single tickets from Aylesbury to Quainton Road which were printed LNER. We went by train to Quainton Road.

On the way we noticed that the platforms of Waddesdon Station were still there but overgrown. The building had been completely removed. The line to the milk dock on the 'down' had been taken up but the brickwork was in position. It was very overgrown.

At Quainton Road it was especially noticed that the old Metropolitan boards were still in their original condition. White letters on a red background probably the only ones left. These were on both platforms but were not in use. The station appeared little changed except that there were no full size name boards.

We walked to Quainton Road Junction by road and then went down to the Verney line north of the bridge.

The whole of the line to Verney Junction was walked over except using the road between the Lee and occupation bridges. The 'down' line had been removed from Quainton Road junction to a point between Winslow Road and Verney Junction (approx 49$^7/_8$ miles from Baker Street). It was noticed how gradually the main LNER line diverged from the Verney line. Most of the trespass notices were headed 'Metn. Gt Cen. Rly' although there were a few of the more usual 'Met & GC Joint Committee'.

The line to Lee Bridge is mostly on a slight embankment. Lee Bridge (MR 189) is a single span of brick. About 100 yards, to the south a wire fence had been placed across the line which was easily removable should the line be used.

From Lee Bridge a road was parallel to the line for about half a mile and on the

[1] Quainton Road to Verney Junction was converted to single track on January 28, 1940. The remaining Verney line was removed from Junction to Winslow Road in 1949.

same level. After this the line runs in a cutting to a point north of Hogshaw Bridge. About quarter of a mile south of the occupation bridge (the boundary of Quainton and Hogshaw parishes) a footpath crosses the line and there is another wire fence across the line.

The line was rejoined at the Occupation bridge (MR 191), three spans built of brick, which carries a footpath from Quainton to Botolph Claydon. A quarter mile north is Hogshaw Bridge (MR 192) similarly built. On the 'down' side to the north of Hogshaw Bridge near mile post 47¼ there is a distant signal with a post of concrete with dates 23.6.31 and entirely unconnected.

A variety of rail chairs were in use north of Quainton Road Junction. This we noticed had several identification names, GCR (various dates up to 1923), LNER (up to 1939) MSLR (1892), GW & GC Jt (1905)

At Granborogh Road station there had been a couple of sidings with loading dock south of the roadway, whilst the station was to the north, the railway crossing on the level. The station buildings had been removed and also the footbridge (MR 194)), only the brick supports being left in position. The platforms were overgrown so much so that sheep were actually grazing on them!

A little to the south of the road were some LNER goods wagons. These extended continuously northward to Verney Junction, a distance of 2¼ miles. The occupant of the railway cottage on the 'up' side at Granborough Road told us that these wagons were awaiting repair and that a couple of years before had extended southwards to Quainton Road Junction, a distance of six miles! The line had been closed to goods traffic about 1947 and this traffic diverted via the spur north of Calvert.

About a mile north of Grandborough Road station where a footpath crosses the railway there was an empty railway cottage. It was once occupied by an LNER permanent way man. He now lives at the former Stationmaster's house at Winslow Road. This now an empty cottage that once obtained its water supply about three times a week in milk churns unloaded from the train. A small platform was erected for this purpose.

We were asked into the cottage at Winslow Road station which is on the 'up' side of the line. The man living there had worked on the railway for 36 years.

Winslow Road station, which is immediately south of the road was in a similar condition to Grandbrough Road.

Continuing on to Verney Junction we found the former 'down' line in position from 49⁷/8 miles and used as a siding.

South of Verney Junction the line curves to the west, crosses over a road (MR 198) and joins the LMS line from Bletchley to Oxford.

Verney Yard cabin is near the road bridge but was out of use and derelict. The extensive siding accommodation appeared little used. The line of wagons finished a little to the east of the station. Verney station box was closed, although it may be opened when required, while the engine dock and water tank and other installations seemed to be out of use. The Stationmaster's House bore the date 1870(LNWR). All station notice boards were LMS and the overbridge carried an LNWR number. The station nameboard was standard LMS type. The 50½ milepost from Baker Street was situated to the west of the station in the yard.

Looking south north of the junction at Quainton. On the left the bridge of the Aylesbury & Buckingham Railway. The new GCR bridge obviously under construction which would make the period likely at 1897-8.

Leicestershire County Council

Winslow Road station looking north during the period of the Metropolitan with a D class engine no 73 introduced 1895 until withdrawn in 1920. They were intended to work the lines north of Aylesbury. A very strange train with a mixed assembly of goods wagons and a passenger coach.

QRS Collection

On Monday 6 we took the bus from Aylesbury to Kingswood and walked southwards to the site of the terminus of Church Siding. The siding was just traceable here. The traces were soon lost until we reached a field to the south east of Yeat Farm where there appeared to have been two additional sidings as well as the main Church Siding. The traces were completely lost again through ploughing. The siding is known to have turned southwards towards Wotton Underwood. Nearly half a mile north of Wotton

The Metropolitan signalbox at the junction north of the station looking from the A&BR side which has obviously been relaid with bull head rail replacing earlier bridge rail.

Leicestershire County Council

One of the huge 'K' class 2-6-4 tanks in the 'down' yard at Quainton.

Park became very clear, but much overgrown, and traced to the Park boundary. In the Park the site was less clear. The last part where the siding joined the Brill branch is now a path leading to the village. The base of the water tank in an adjoining field in the direction of Wotton Row.

Aylesbury station locomotive shed in the late 1940's with a Great Western tank engine. These would be used on trains on the former Wycombe Railway branch to Aylesbury.

QRS Collection

The profile of the GCR survived on the line passing through Quainton many years after its amalgamation. One of the Robinson Atlantics seen here at Aylesbury immediately post second world war. Note the early footbridge at Aylesbury.

QRS Collection

From this point to Wotton station the course of the line was an asphalt path and east of Wotton Station under the railway bridge it became concrete road leading to the RP depot as previously mentioned. The road was followed for about ¾ mile to the east as far as the entrance to the depot. After a detour the Brill branch was again picked up at Westcott and the junction of Westcott siding was visible.

One of the Standard class Fives 4-6-0 no 73159 which took over the Sheffield trains in the 1950's. Prior to this after the withdrawal of the original GCR locomotives in the immediate post war period the service was operated by the LNER B17 class of football club named locomotives. These were joined by V2 2-6-2, Pacifics and B1 engines.

Andrew Bratton

Aylesbury with a southbound train hauled by one of the Britannia class no 70015 'Apollo' in the 1950's.

Andrew Bratton

The exploration of the Brill branch had to be brought to a close at this point. Altogether a most enjoyable and rewarding weekend.

Written on February 15, 1955 from a report written just after the visit.

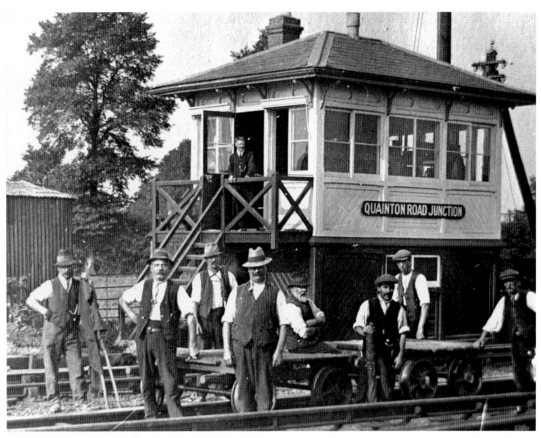

Permanent way gang working outside Quainton Road Junction signalbox early in the twentieth century.

QRS Collection

The ticket office at the entrance to Verney Junction station probably quite new after the rebuilding of the station by the Metropolitan in 1898.

QRS Collection

Two gentlemen in what could be described as clerical attire attending to some permanent way matter at Verney Junction. As the signalbox and Metropolitan Stationmaster's house have been built it must be assumed to be early in the twentieth century.

A Metropolitan E class no L45 at Aylesbury on August 11, 1956. The sister engine L44 was purchased by QRS and re-stored from the London Transport livery as seen here to original Metropolitan livery and is now part of the collection.

R C Riley

The line from Quainton to Verney Junction was withdrawn from passenger service in 1936. It continued in freight use with LNER and British Railways Eastern Region goods working up until the late 1950's. It was used for a time for storage of passenger coaches awaiting repair at Wolverton Works, also wagons, before it was lifted altogether in the mid 1960's.

R C Casserley

The view north on a rather poor print but the sense of speed of this northbound train gives it a presence. Also the view of the ground between Aylesbury and Quainton shows how the line looked for many years until it became no longer neccessary to hold back the vegetation.

In the north looking back to Aylesbury in the late 1940's from the Thame Road bridge giving a view of the goods yard. The 'gallows' structure on the siding on the right is a loading gauge.

At Aylesbury looking north as a Robinson Atlantic no 5265 waits to depart.

QRS Collection

The Aylesbury yard north of the station in 1946. The cattle dock platform in the foreground was the original broad gauge goods shed. Some time in the early decades of the twentieth century a new shed was built a little further north.

QRS Collection

A Metropolitan train north of Harrow hauled by an A class engine. There is a suggestion of new works with the bridge and temporary track in the foreground. After 1910 electrification from Baker street to Harrow and Uxbridge steam continued on the north section.

QRS Collection

The role of ex-GCR Atlantics was taken over with LNER B17 classes as in the view of no 2862 *Manchester United.*
QRS Collection

The looking south from no 2 platform early in the twentieth century. Thanks to the past and present QRS members so little has changed. The footbridge was condemned by British Railways as unsafe shortly after the QRS took over the station. Not to be defeated the members hired a crane that lifted the bridge onto the 'down' platform during an engineering possession of the line. They then rebuilt the deck of the bridge using modern welded construction and rivetted the lattice sides back on. This was all approved by BR and the bridge remains perfectly sound to this day.

One of the C class engines likely to be in the Vale of Aylesbury en route for Verney Junction with a train of early rigid 8-wheel coaches and the essential milk van close to the engine. A very early 4-wheel vehicle (c1869) is included second from the end. It is a remarkable thought to visualise this train standing at the patform at Quainton and finally completing its journey at the country oupost of Verney Junction

QRS Collection

Quainton station looking north looking from the signalbox shortly before closure with signals pulled off for an 'up' train. Notably, still a Metropolitan signal.

P. Clarke

Beyond 1936

The poet W H Auden called the thirties 'a low dishonest decade'. Certainly large scale unemployment, the rise of fascism in Spain with the squalid appeasement solution to the Munich agreement would support that. Yet the famous poet did write the successful film poem 'Night Mail' and Walt Disney premiered his beautiful hand drawn film *Snow White* in 1937, unmatchable by any computer.

The closure of the Brill Tramway, was not without its own story book quality. Also the ending of passenger services to Verney Junction reduced the role of Quainton Road with five 'down' trains stopping and seven 'up' trains, with only two on Sundays. In 1910, the year of the introduction of the Pullman service it had eleven return workings to Baker Street.

With the outbreak of the World War Two the site was one of many chosen by the Ministry of Food in country places with rail or canal access for the storage of food supplies and also as a depot for fuel supplies for Westcott airfield. The result was that six Romney huts were built in 1942 with brick buildings using the metals of 'up' yard and the Brill line as a siding connection. The brick buildings were for 2000 tons of flour and made vermin proof. The Romney huts held 1500 tons of sugar. The buildings were built up on hard core bases of bomb damage rubble brought by rail from London.

In all probability there would have been a military presence at the station to prevent pilferage as there was a high black market demand for rationed food.

With the end of hostilities prisoners of war were brought back to Westcott Airfield for release. Some 53,000 men were flown into the airfield and issued with travel warrants. A certain number would probably get lifts to Aylesbury but no doubt some of the number would come to Quainton Road. It is impossible to imagine how they must have felt, the trauma of battle, the lasting ignominy of being taken prisoner with

27

Quainton Road station looking south shortly before closure. Note the coaches stored in both yards en route to Wolverton.
P. Clarke

the privations of the camps. Then in a few days, to be sitting on a seat on a typical English country station waiting for a train home.

The station would have provided a useful role in the establishing of the airfield both in bringing the material and providing transport for the arriving and departing of crews. It was used for the training of bomber crews for Halifax's, Wellingtons and Lancasters. Sadly some came to grief in crashes nearby.

It was relinquished by the RAF in August 1945 becoming a guided projectile research establishment in April 1946. So the service uniforms at the station would be replaced with scientific boffins in chalky sports coats

The MoF buildings at the station remained in use by the government until the 1960's when it was considered the floors were not sufficiently supported for the regular use of the more successful warehouse carriers, the fork lift trucks. They certainly proved very robust when the task of cutting into them to allow for railway tracks had to be done by the Quainton Railway Society!

After the ending of the war the much used ex-GCR main line that ran through the station came under scrutiny, along with much of the railway system which had suffered badly during the war, whilst providing the essential means of winning it. With little investment, apart from essential military logistic needs. The extra heavy traffic left many miles of permanent way badly worn exceeding renewal dates. A new appraisal of traction policy brought new steam locomotive designs rather than the transformation to alternative modern traction that had been evident in the thinking of the companies before the war. It was a delay that lead to confusion and some disarray a few years later.

The entire railway system required massive investment if it was to serve the nation in a future central transport role.

The Brill platform no 3 with road access directly to it which is now tarmacadam driveway.

Railway nationalisation in 1948 ensured that investment would be under government control. How the former group companies could have managed a recovery to the standards of pre-war, will never be known. It is very likely that some of them would have wanted to promote alternative traction earlier. The LMS had shown this with their diesel policy.

The government established the British Transport Commission with the illusory ideal that all things could be resolved into a single purpose. The BTC established a Railway Executive to look after the railway side of things. These men of the former private companies set about establishing a brand new fleet of steam locomotives containing all the advantages culled from all the experiences of the former companies through the years. Glowing publicity brought the publics' attention to these examples of the finest ideals in engine design naming a class 'Britannia'. They were also doomed to be the shortest locomotive lives in history, many engines had barely rolled off the production lines to be soon withdrawn. This underlies the fact that it may well have been best to build more of the established steam engines like the Black Five as an interim and introduce new power earlier. In fairness it has to be admitted that the modernisation plan of 1954 had borne some fruit of new traction concepts with the first diesel multiple unit from Marylebone to Aylesbury entering service from January 23, 1961. Previously an experiment had taken place with single unit diesel railcars between Banbury, Buckingham and Bletchley in 1956.

It had also been recognised by town planners that Britain aspired to be a car owning democracy. A legacy of the War, like the first World War had enabled many soldiers to learn to drive during their military service and were now looking for jobs. This gave impetus in the post war recovery to more investment in developing of road transport services. In 1956 the first motorway type road was opened around Preston in Lancashire the M6, this was followed with another short section around Lancaster.

A view south of the station with coal hoppers in the siding now used for the rides train. Extant is the former Metropolitan signal box that was demolished as sale of the site to the LRPS was being completed. Understating the point, it is difficult to comprehend this as anything but a negative response to the preservation movement.

P. Clarke

The opening of the M1 motorway, a complete major trunk route between London and Birmingham took place in November 1959.

The thorny subject of under investment in the railways came in 1963 with the publication of the famous Beeching plan *The Reshaping of British Railways* which became a shocking revelation as it closed and proposed removal of the ex-GCR main line north of Claydon Junction. As parliament accepted the recommendations of the doctor the voices of protest were left winnowing on the wind as the Department of Transport was determined that these proposals should be acted upon.

It has to be admitted that the former companies had started closing lines before World War II and had they returned it is very likely that they would have continued to do so. In the thirties a daily road van carrying parcels went from Buckingham to Bletchley operated by the LMS.

By early 1966 removal of the former GCR line was well underway, a line that would have provided some interesting advantages had it survived to the present day.

The end of the steam locomotive itself took place some two years later in 1968, Quainton Road would have become a rather sad derelict place but for the Quainton Railway Society who arrived on site in 1967. It appeared at the time that the nation's railways were diminishing on a scale that had never been imagined, and for those people that believed in them as a mode of transport and historical interest it was alarming to witness.

Consequently people with energy and foresight formed together in like-minded groups to see what could be done to retain some of the heritage of a great age. One of these was the London Railway Preservation Society that met in 1960. This followed on from the autonomous body of the Railway Preservation Society from which it grew as an offshoot; a London branch was established in 1962. On April 14, 1962 an Extraordinary General Meeting with Noel Draycott in the chair was held, with secretary Mr R A Castle, Noel Draycott was also Treasurer.

Crucially membership built up, bringing with it the inexhaustible energy that would

What a fine response to enthusiasm of the 1950's a *Railway World* railtour calling at Quainton with the preserved E class complete with Metropolitan coaches.

QRS Collection

be needed as some funds were scraped together to purchase relics and rolling stock before these pieces of history went to the breaker's torch or the scrapyard bonfire.

The then Ministry of Food was approached and permission was obtained to store the Society relics on the sidings of two disused refrigerated food stores (built during the war in the same system as the ones at Quainton but refrigerated) at Luton and Bishops Stortford. It soon became obvious that the sidings were insufficient to hold all that was been acquired in the expanding collection. Also the MoF discovered that there was a commercial demand for the sidings so the Society was under notice to find a permanent site.

Roy Miller and Peter Clarke had by this time purchased their first steam locomotive 41298 and were looking for a permanent site. Within a very short time both were elected onto the LRPS Executive Committee and given the task of finding a suitable site for a railway centre.

In January 1966 the LRPS searched earnestly to find a permanent site to store these acquisitions which at that time were held temporarily in various locations. Such was the immediate need to claim objects from extinction what siding space that had been begged or hired soon became entirely full. Secretary R A Castle at the Third Annual General Meeting on the January 31, 1967 made it plain that something had to be done soon.

So it was with no little urgency that members Roy Miller and Peter Clarke girded themselves with the task of finding somewhere for the Society to become firmly established with all its stock combined. It is a great credit to them that they took on this task which must at the very least seemed daunting.

The 'down' yard at Quainton as it looked shortly before occupation by the LRPS. This is how it would have looked for the wartime period of the Ministry of Food depot.

QRS Collection

The view as above looking south.

QRS Collection

Nearly a year was spent looking and considering disused railway sites in the home counties. Eventually Quainton Road was chosen as being an historical railway junction on a little used railway line with plenty of land and the potential of purchasing a length of line (into Aylesbury) when funds permitted. Another consideration was its distance from houses that may be offended by the smoke and noise of steam locomotives.[1]

Quainton Road station was spared loss to the system by being on a section of line to Claydon that was still being used by the London Brick Company at Calvert.

On January 1. 1969 it was reported that British Railways Board agreed to the sale of the land at this station after lengthy negotiations. The completion of this was commendable requiring understanding all round of what the Society wished to do

[1] Planning applications on 'up' yard at Quainton dated January 27, 1967.

The Aylesbury Joint shed with its significantly individual coal and water structure assemblies.

QRS COllection

Soon after the restoration of the A3 Pacific *Flying Scotsman* to LNER livery by the new owner Alan Pegler it did a special run from Leicester to Marylebone on the former Great Central Railway main line on June 15, 1963. The special was organised by the Railway Preservation Society. It is seen here at Aylesbury having passed through Quainton Road.

Brian Sessions

Metropolitan A class engine at Aylesbury on a goods train. Still with the condensing pipes used for underground working, no. 23 worked on the Brill branch and is now the only engine of this class preserved in the Transport for London Museum Collection at Covent Garden.

QRS Collection

The branch from Princes Risborough to Aylesbury happily survived the worst effects of the sixties closures and is still in use. Here one of the Collett 5700 class 0-6-0 pannier tanks that worked the push-pull trains in the 1950's is seen at Aylesbury. One of the class is held in the collection at the Buckinghamshire Railway Centre.

QRS Collection

---An 'up' line push-pull train working to Aylesbury passing through Quainton Road in the early 1960's. hauled by a former GWR pannier tank. This working appears to be unusual and I am indebted to Andrew Bratton (QRS) who was able to provide the details. A daily trip from Aylesbury to Calvert of the Banbury/Princes Risborough/Aylesbury push-pull. Timings: Aylesbury 5.20, Quainton Road 5.30, Calvert 5.38. Return Calvert 6.15, Quainton Road 6.23, Aylesbury 6.33. The photograph is obviously the return working.
QRS Collection

Britannia class 70054 'Dornoch Firth' heads hurriedly past the Quainton Road signalbox in the early 1960's.
Andrew Bratton

beyond just being well intentioned railway enthusiasts. The 'down' yard and platform became owned by the Society on April 1, 1969.

What transpired as a freehold purchase which was to prove crucial to decisions and developments made in subsequent years.

Very quickly coaches and wagons were moved from sidings at Luton and Bishops Stortford. These included the Locomotive L44 (No 1), the Wolverton Dining car and another LNWR coach. They had to be stored at Aylesbury to await the severed connection into the sidings at Quainton being restored. Some other preserved pieces also came by road.

Once managed it was not a sight for the faint hearted, with everything needing much work to make completion. Also, and crucially, the stock was in the open. The prospects that lay ahead must have been visually overwhelming and it says much for the working members of the time that they remained undaunted and took the positive view that now, at last, they had a place to work without worry of eviction.

Clarke/QRS Collection

Looking north at Aylesbury in the 1930's.

Throughout the 1970's the Quainton Railway Society were able to make use of the main running line on Bank Holiday weekends when a DMU shuttle service would operate between Aylesbury and the station.

The Years of Consolidation 1966-1980

This period started in a frenzy as British Railways moved apace from early in the decade sending locomotives to the scrapyard towards their dateline of August 11, 1968 when steam would end on the national system. It was a twilight of the gods as they were drawn in pathetic trains to various scrapyards, British Railways being more than pleased to see the back of them. In south Wales at Cashmores and on Barry Island scrap merchant Dai Woodham must have been more then pleased to see them arrive! He soon realised that he had moved from executioner to re-sale dealer as societies were quickly formed to promote their rescue and restoration. It has to be said that what was achieved in a very short period was a kind of locomotive 'Dunkirk' with many more being rescued than was imagined possible at the outset. Many of them finding sanctuary at Quainton.

The former Great Central line at Quainton ceased passenger service on September 5, 1966. The next station north at Calvert had closed in March 1963.

In order to generate funds as soon as possible on August 8 1969 Bank Holiday the site made its first official opening with a steam weekend and two locomotives working 'Juno' and 'Sir Thomas'. There were also two working signals in place.

Anthea Hanscomb recalls:

'The newly formed Signal & Telegraph Department installed a simple signalling system in the Down Yard, including a barrier to protect the pedestrian crossing. Over the next few years, Mike (Hanscomb) and his colleagues developed the system to provide two signalling locations, Quainton Station and Quainton South, with tokenless

A fine celebratory note could be struck when a celebrity would attend steaming days. Here Don Estelle one of the stars of the BBC television series 'It Ain't 'half Hot Mum' enjoys the experience of riding on the footplate of Met 1.
QRS Collection

'block' working between them. This enabled operation of two trains in the 'Down Yard' (one travelling up the single line while the other shunted at the station), which was of great interest to members and visitors alike."

Having established a permanent site more acquisitions were gained throughout the year. The Hudswell Clark 0-6-0 tank engine 'Sir Thomas' of the Oxfordshire Ironstone Company was presented to the Society. In 1969 it was fitted with a vacuum brake at Quainton, also one railcar and two carriages. The Society also provided sanctuary for various locomotives and stock before moving on to other railway preservation societies with temporary accommodation after being rescued from the scrapyards

In 1970 Quainton Railway Society Ltd was formed to give legal protection to members and to ensure the future preservation of historical vehicles the LRPS owned. In September 1970 the British Railways track was slewed and joined to a spur from the 'down' yard to bring in the stock that was stored at Aylesbury.

The Signalling & Telegraph Committee worked hard to improve signalling. Steve Clark designed the control panel at the station. The signalling was changed for two train running in 1971.

By 1975 a most important advantage was accomplished with storage track under cover. As all societies involved with restoration are aware of the need to shelter standing vehicles from the weather. Under this, one of the first vehicles to be worked on

The 1970's was a pioneering time and after many difficulties it was a welcome relief to see the public support the efforts to retain that for which many people held affection for by visiting the site. This train has just brought visitors from Aylesbury.

QRS Collection

was the Wolverton Dining Car. Work also began on 'Wightwick Hall'. Also the Beattie well tank (1874) that was restored as Southern Railway E0134 in gloss black.

The Society purchased the track in the 'up' yard some time before the purchase of the land to prevent it being taken up and sold for scrap. Eventually the land was purchased in two stages to accommodate the coal merchant then on site. It would have been possible to include the station building but BR insisted that the station canopy would have to be removed. This would of course have destroyed an important feature of the station, so BR retained ownership of the building itself and the 'up' platforms and do to this day.

In March 1976 negotiations for the purchase of the 'up' yard from British Rail were completed. This meant that the Society owned both 'up and 'down 'yards. The Beattie Well tank was successfully used and steamed on bank holidays.

In April the Society had managed to open on eight occasions for the public.

By the end of the 1976 season, the Down Yard signalling system (see diagram on page 56) had become life-expired, and the decision was taken to remove the equipment and to operate the line on the 'One Engine in Steam' system, which is perfectly adequate for the simple train movements. The Signal & Telegraph members then turned their attention to staging signalling demonstrations, and a very successful exhibition "Sigex 77" was held during the 1977 open days.

One of the early open days where apprehension was replaced with joyful satisfaction as many people came to view the exhibits. It was a relief to many members of the public that the steam operated railway so beloved to many was not gone from sight forever. The Wolverton Diner is still in its pink undercoat. The tracks on which people are walking are those of the former Brill branch.

QRS Collection

In 1979 the site was able to provide enlightenment for youngsters with the attendance of 1400 school children to watch locomotive steamings and manoeuvres. Such visits have happily continued to the present day. On this 10th Anniversary year of the working site it could now claim that it held the largest collection of steam locomotives in the country.

In 1980 a interesting and potentially expanding source of revenue was discovered when the site provided a film set for the pop group 'The Tourists' singing 'Good to be back home'. Also Granada's 'Jewel in the Crown' production and many others that required atmosphere from railways.

In the mid-1980's the former Harlington (Beds) signalbox was acquired and erected in a commanding position overlooking the Down Yard. Various schemes have been mooted for signalling to be controlled from this 40-lever box, or for the creation of a signalling demonstration to entertain and educate the visitors. It is a prospect awaiting undertaking and completion.

In 1988 Roy Miller was made a full time employee with his appointment as the Centre's new Curator. A pleasing trend was that the Centre was able to report a 15% growth of visitors from 1987.

These photographs in this section show events of the historic day of September 23, 1970 when Quainton first took stock onto the site. This was thoughtfully recorded by Tim Stevens to whom I am indebted for the use of them. The effort is clearly evident and worthy of lasting portrayal. The slewing of British Rail track was of course undertaken by their own employees.

Tim Stevens

The stock arrives from Aylesbury looking a little sad but at last - home!

The engine in charge of bringing the stock from Aylesbury was D5240 a type 2 Bo-Bo diesel. The class was first introduced in 1958.

Tim Stevens

Having arrived on site the train cannot pass onto the metals of the Society but has to be hauled from the arrival point by a Society engine. This noble task fell to the earliest working engine of the Society, the tank engine of the former North Oxfordshire Ironstone Railway 'Sir Thomas'. The engine may now rest as a static unsteamable exhibit but its efforts were to serve the Society well that day.

Tim Stevens

One of the prized acquisitions the Wolverton Dining Car in a pink undercoat. It is remarkable to see the vehicle as it is now in the Rewley Road station building superbly restored.

Tim Stevens

At this point L44 the Metropolitan E class waits to be brought in still standing with the diesel.

Tim Stevens

Slowly the coaches are shunted into the long siding.

Tim Stevens

The type 2 at that time a conspicuous newcomer to the British Railway scene, now, itself consigned to history.

Tim Stevens

A rare mix of history and motive power.

Tim Stevens

British Railways brake van is returned to the diesel.

Tim Stevens

'Sir Thomas' leaves to join the waiting diesel.

TIm Stevens

'Sir Thomas' at rest, the day's work now completed.

Time Stevens

'Sir Thomas' arrives at its new home having been donated from the Oxfordshire Ironstone Company. It would soon be put to work at Quainton hauling in the stock arriving on site.

P Clarke

A remarkable locomotive similar to the first engine used on the Wotton Tramway built by Aveling Porter.

Andrew Bratton

Many uniqe locomotives have visited Quainton as this design introduced in 1878 on the Midland Railway of an 0-6-0 tank engine. It was withdrawn from service in 1966 and is now held at the Barrow Hill Roundhouse.

Andrew Bratton

The Society were able to provide accommodation to GWR interests with the restoration of *King Edward I* that was completed in the 'Kings Shed'. It operated on the opposite end of a steam special with *Nunney Castle*. Other notable locomotives that found temporary sanctuary at Quainton were West Country 4-6-2 no 34016 *Bodmin* which went on to exemplary service on special trains after leaving the site in 1976. It now resides on the Mid Hants Railway.

Another locomotive was the Standard class 4 2-6-0 no 76017 which left the site in 1978 also now on the Mid Hants Railway. A class 25 diesel also was temporarily housed at Quainton no 25 057 (D5207) that left in 1991.

Andrew Bratton

A group photograph for the album taken in the summer of 1970. Presenting the new acquisition of 'Sir Thomas'.

A chronology of locomotives arriving at and departing from Quainton Road from 1969 to date banded in black

Locomotive	1963	1964	1965	1966	1967	1968	1969	1970	1971	1972	1973
4-8-4 South A no 3405											
2-8-2T 7200											
4-6-0 Wightwick Hall											
4-6-0 King Edward I											■
2-6-2T Ivatt 41298							■	■	■	■	■
2-6-2T Ivatt 41313								■	■	■	■
2-6-0 Ivatt 46447										■	■
0-6-0T Sir Thomas 1334							■	■	■	■	■
0-6-0ST Juno 3850							■	■	■	■	■
0-6-0ST Cunarder 47160							■	■	■	■	■
0-6-0PT GWR 4450								■	■	■	■
0-6-0PT GWR 7715								■	■	■	■
0-6-0PT GWR 9466								■	■	■	■
0-6-0ST Chislet 2498								■	■	■	■
0-6-0T Coventry No 1									■	■	■
0-6-0ST NCB 64											
0-6-0ST Robert 2068								■	■	■	■
0-6-0ST Austerity 3890							■	■	■	■	■
0-6-0ST Arthur 3782											
0-6-0T Midland 1708					■	■	■	■	■	■	■
2-4-0WT Beattie 314	■	■	■	■	■	■	■				
0-4-4T Met 1	■	■	■	■	■	■	■				
0-4-0ST Swanscombe							■	■	■	■	■
0-4-0ST AB Alexander							■	■	■	■	■
0-4-0ST AB Punch Hull 776							■	■	■	■	■
0-4-0T LNER 985		■	■	■	■	■	■	■	■	■	■
0-4-0ST MW 1795							■	■	■	■	■
0-4-0 Holy War 779								■	■	■	■
0-4-0ST 3717 HL								■	■	■	■
0-4-0ST Millom 1749								■	■	■	■
4-wheel Sentinel 11 4366								■	■	■	■
0-4-0 Sentinel 9537											
0-4-0 Sentinel 6515										■	■
0-4-0 Sentinel 9376									■	■	■
0-4-0 AB Fireless 2243											
0-4-0 AB Fireless 1477					■	■	■	■	■	■	■
0-4-0 AB Fireless 1562						■	■	■	■	■	■
0-4-0ST AB Tom Parry											
0-4-0ST Miranda/Gibralter											
0-4-0ST AB 1865 Alexander				■	■	■	■	■	■	■	■
0-4-0ST Bagnall 2469				■	■	■	■	■	■	■	■
0-4-0T Neilson 4444				■	■	■	■				
0-4-0ST Hunslet 287											
0-4-0WT AP Sydenham 3567			■	■	■	■	■	■	■	■	■
0-4-0ST AB 2015			■	■	■	■	■	■	■	■	■
0-4-0ST Trym 287		■	■								
Steam Railcar S-M 5208											
0-4-0T Peckett 1900											
0-4-0ST 1742						■	■	■	■	■	■
Diesel Locomotives											
0-6-0 DM Lord Wenlock											
Kerr Stuart 4428							■	■	■	■	■
Petrol Railcar 9040							■	■	■	■	■
5207											
0-6-0 DH Hunslet 7016											
0-4-0 DM Osram 20067									■	■	■
0-4-0 DM Hibberd 2102											
0-4-0 DM Hilsea 463153											
0-4-0 DM Hunslet 2067											
0-4-0 DM Bag Drewery 2161											
0-4-0 DM Ker/Huns Redland K4428							■	■	■	■	■
0-4-0 Sentinel 24											
Walrus											
Hibberd DM 3765											

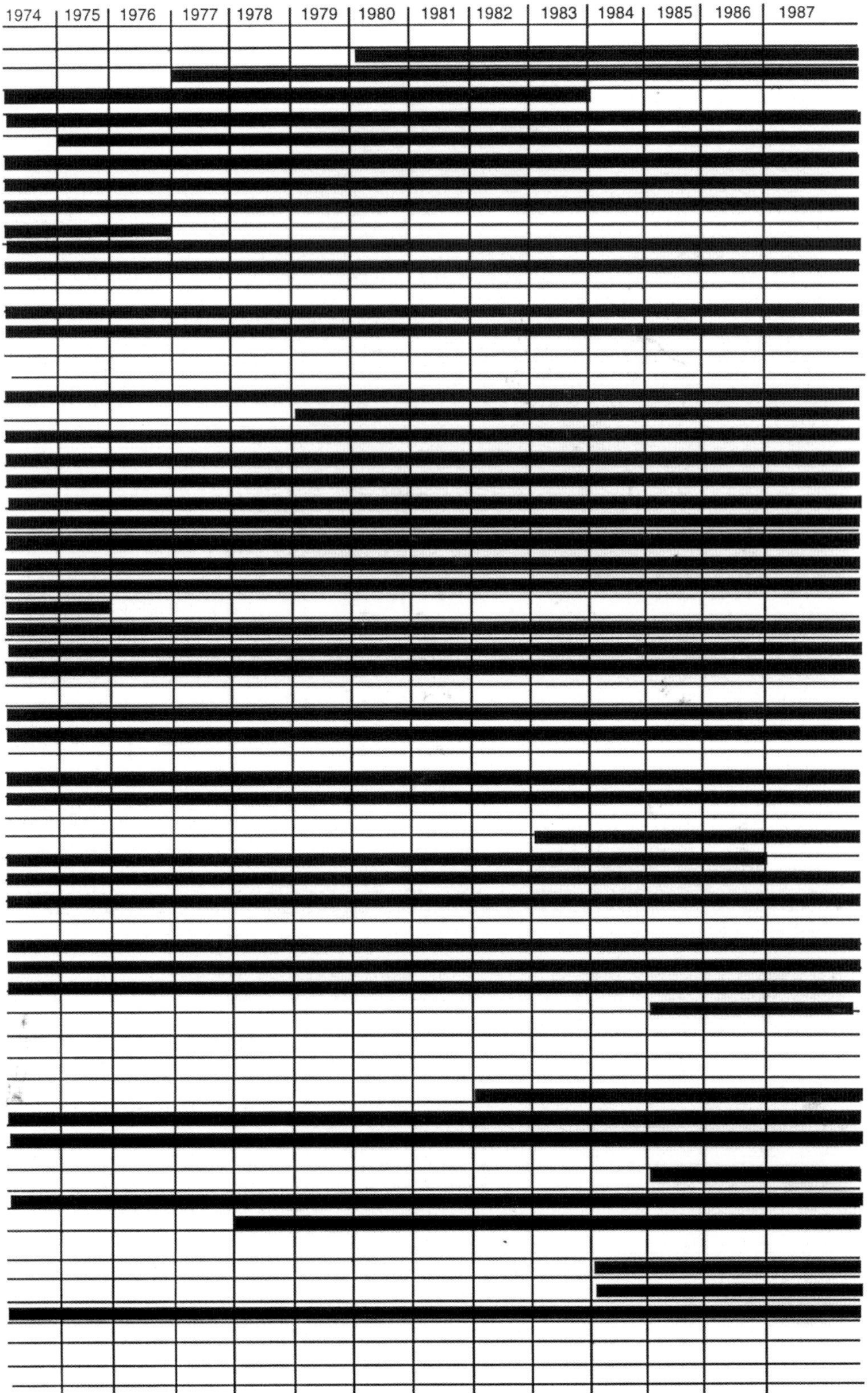
1974
1975
1976
1977
1978
1979
1980
1981
1982
1983
1984
1985
1986
1987

Locomotive	1988	1989	1990	1991	1992	1993	1994	1995	1996	1997
4-8-4 South A no 3405				■	■	■	■	■	■	■
2-8-2T 7200	■	■	■	■	■	■	■	■	■	■
4-6-0 Wightwick Hall	■	■	■	■	■	■	■	■	■	■
4-6-0 King Edward I	■	■								
2-6-2T Ivatt 41298	■	■	■	■	■	■	■	■	■	■
2-6-2T Ivatt 41313	■	■	■	■	■	■	■	■	■	■
2-6-0 Ivatt 46447	■	■	■	■	■	■	■	■	■	■
0-6-0T Sir Thomas 1334	■	■	■	■	■	■	■	■	■	■
0-6-0ST Juno 3850	■	■	■	■	■	■	■	■	■	■
0-6-0ST Cunarder										
0-6-0PT GWR 4450										
0-6-0PT GWR 7715	■	■	■	■	■	■	■	■	■	■
0-6-0PT GWR 9466	■	■	■	■	■	■	■	■	■	■
0-6-0ST Chislet 2498										
0-6-0T Coventry No 1	■	■	■	■	■	■	■	■	■	■
0-6-0ST NCB 64										
0-6-0ST Robert 2068										
0-6-0ST Austerity 3890										
0-6-0ST Arthur 3782										
0-6-0T Midland 1708										
2-4-0WT Beattie 314	■	■	■	■	■	■	■	■	■	■
0-4-4T Met 1	■	■	■	■	■	■	■	■	■	■
0-4-0ST Swanscombe	■	■	■	■	■	■	■	■	■	■
0-4-0ST AB Alexander										
0-4-0ST AB Punch Hull										
0-4-0T LNER 985										
0-4-0ST MW 1795										
0-4-0 Holy War										
0-4-0ST 3717 HL										
0-4-0ST Millom 1749	■	■	■	■	■	■	■	■	■	■
4-wheel Sentinel 11 4366										
0-4-0 Sentinel 9537										
0-4-0 Sentinel 6515										
0-4-0 Sentinel 9376	■	■	■	■	■	■	■			
0-4-0 AB Fireless 2243										
0-4-0 AB Fireless 1477										
0-4-0 AB Fireless 1562										
0-4-0ST AB Tom Parry		■	■	■	■	■	■	■	■	■
0-4-0ST Miranda/Gibralter	■	■	■	■	■	■	■	■	■	■
0-4-0ST AB 1865										
0-4-0ST Bagnall 2469										
0-4-0T Neilson 4444										
0-4-0ST Hunslet 287										
0-4-0WT AP Sydenham 3567										
0-4-0ST AB 2015										
0-4-0ST Trym 287	■	■								
Steam Railcar S-M 5208										
0-4-0T Peckett 1900										
0-4-0ST 1742										
Diesel Locomotives										
0-6-0 DM Lord Wenlock										
Kerr Stuart 4428										
Petrol Railcar 9040	■	■	■	■	■	■	■	■	■	■
Esso Loco 2161										
Esso Loco 2067										
5207										
0-6-0 DH Hunslet 7016	■	■	■							
0-4-0 DM Osram 20067										
0-4-0 DM Hibberd 2102										
0-4-0 DM Hilsea 463153										
0-4-0 DM Hunslet 2067										
0-4-0 DM Bag Drewery 2161	■	■	■	■	■	■	■	■	■	■
0-4-0 DM Ker/Huns Redland K4428										
0-4-0 Sentinel 24	■	■	■	■	■					

| 1998 | 1999 | 2000 | 2001 | 2002 | 2003 | 2004 | 2005 | 2006 | 2007 | 2008 | 2009 | 2010 | |

The precise art of restoration. Above the former LNWR Sleeping Car (1904) converted by the LMS to a cinema coach in 1936 photographed at Quainton in on July 25, 2001. Below is the vehicle totally restored in 2004 and now serving as the Cinema Coach in Rewley Road station building.

Both photographs by Lance Adlam

As early as 1970 the Society were able to convey passengers in a novel way in open trucks. The former LT pannier is seen here on the no 3 platform.

Andrew Bratton

Under clear signals 'Sir Thomas' provides the evocative whiffs of steam and burning coal that indescribably relates to many personal experiences.

John H Bird

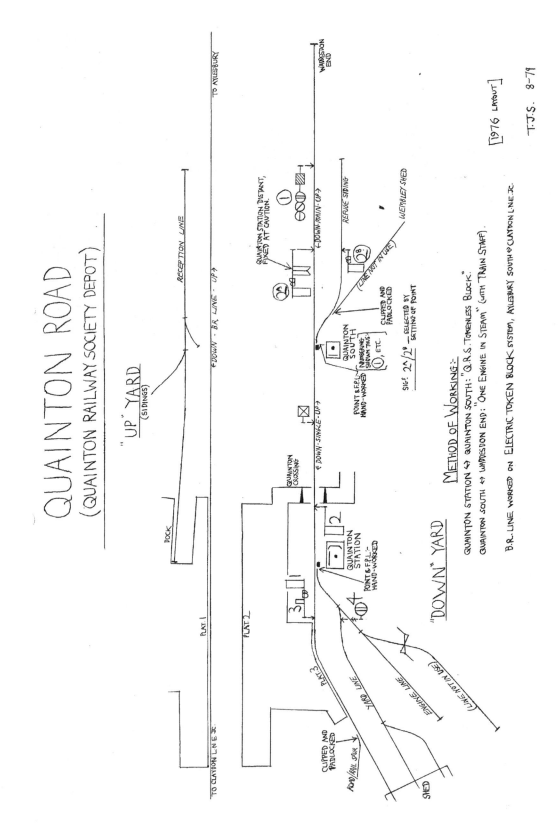

QUAINTON ROAD
(QUAINTON RAILWAY SOCIETY DEPOT)

METHOD OF WORKING:-

QUAINTON STATION ⟷ QUAINTON SOUTH: "Q.R.S. TOKENLESS BLOCK."

QUAINTON SOUTH ⟷ WADDESDON END: "ONE ENGINE IN STEAM" (WITH TRAIN STAFF)

B.R. LINE WORKED ON ELECTRIC TOKEN BLOCK SYSTEM, AYLESBURY SOUTH ⟷ CLAYTON L.N.E. JE.

[1976 LAYOUT]

T.J.S. 8-79

A moment between scenes shooting for a production of *Sherlock Holmes* at Quainton. In the group of three men on the right the first man with stick is Peter Cushing, alongside him also with stick is John Mills. The costumes and the train make a fine presentation of the period.

QRS Collection

'Action to the word, word to the Action'

After the station was made derelict in the sixties it was used for a Tom Courtney film called 'Otley'. Subsequently it has 'starred' many times in various feature films and television series right up to the time of writing when it as been used for a demonstration in the BBC television series "Bang Goes the Theory'. It was also used for 'Diamonds Are Forever', 'Woman in Black', 'Dr Who', 'Spooks' and railway scenes for 'Midsomer Murders'.

Many famous people have trod its platforms. Michael Palin, something of an enthusiast himself, stood on number 1 platform for 'Branch line Railway' a BBC production featuring Sir John Betjeman travelling on the Somerset & Dorset Joint Railway branch to Burnham. In 'Metroland' Sir John sat on a seat on number 1 platform describing his lyrical recollections of the Brill train in 1929 ' . . . through oil lit stations'.

Outstandingly a major development came in 1982 when Granada Television negotiated to use its spaciousness for a production of Paul Smith's novel 'The Raj Quartet' to be named as a television series 'Jewel in the Crown'. To facilitate the scenes at

A view of *Coventry* hauling the vintage train in front of the mock Indian station built for the *Jewel in the Crown* production.

J R Fairman

A view along the platform with mock Indian train.

J R Fairman

The platform with covered 'bodies' after the completion of a massacre scene.

J R Fairman

The exterior of the 'Indian' station in the "up' yard.

J R Fairman

Quainton they built two massive outdoor sets in the 'up' yard of an Indian Railway station for the filming. Including four Indian style coaches built on GWR bogies. Members of the Society have recollections of taking their refreshments alongside 'Indian dress' actors in blood stained robes. The two stations appearing in the film were built alongside each other.

Many British international stars appeared in the film working and dining at Quainton, some even joined the Society! In the tradition of Granada productions the series became a major success and is still purchased at the time of writing

A remarkable scene of India created in Buckinghamshire.

Some of the extras forming a crowd on the station between takes.

Quainton continued to receive visitors during the three months of filming, a useful attraction.

QRS Collection

Clever how station detail is arranged to appear randomely placed.

Q RS Collection

The Quainton engine that propelled the trains in 'Jewel in the Crown' but never appeared in the film.

Even the great Charlie Chaplain was portrayed in a film made at the station.

QRS Collection

The Oxford (LNWR) station (Rewley Road) was transferred and completely rebuilt on the site in 1998-99. A very intense and complex process of restoration as the the building was in a poor state when it was taken down.

Greater Developments

In the City of Oxford a contentious issue was the development of the former station site of the LNWR alongside the existing Oxford station. The station site had up until the 1990's been used for a coal yard whilst the station buildings were occupied by the RTS (Regional Tyre Services) and later Budget car rental services. Both these occupations came to an end and much publicity was expressed about the derelict site being a public eyesore. Clearly the situation had to be resolved. The Oxford City wanted the road junction at that point to be redesigned with more space provided as part of the Oxford Transport Strategy. Oxford University on the other hand wanted to make use of the site for a Business School. The problem was of course how to carry out the demolition of a grade II* listed station building that had major historic interest.

The details of the movement of this building to Quainton is published in the book *A Triumph of Restoration* (2008) by Lance Adlam and Bill Simpson, Lamplight Publications. Uniquely Quainton became the site that fulfilled all the parameters insisted upon, important amongst these was the need to have a secure site where the freehold was held by the occupiers.

Plans were placed in hand to remove and restore the building to the Buckinghamshire site. This began in 1998; it was completed in 2000. It was no mean undertaking as the building appeared to be held together mainly by its generations of paintwork!

Also another important event occurred in 2004 solving the problem of the footway link between the 'up' and 'down' yards south of the station. The remedy was spectacularly presented with the installation of a new steel footbridge.

Many locomotives have visited the site, in 1970 West Country pacific 'Bodmin' came

The early days of preservation had many worries and difficulties but there were lighter moments also. Here a group of youngsters sit and pose on the Beattie well tank locomotive in the 1970s. Present day safety regulations would likely prohibit such a grouping.

QRS Collection

in a sadly decrepit condition and left to be restored at the Mid-Hants Railway. Engines visiting in steam have been, amongst many others, 5029 'Nunney Castle', of the same class as 'Defiant'. Others ranged from the replica Stephenson 'Rocket' and the classic outlines of Gresley represented by LNER V2 'Green Arrow' in 2002. Also steaming after its restoration at Quainton, 6024 'King Edward I in 1989. Quainton hosted the Napier Powerex 200 in 2008 to celebrate the Bi-centenary of the foundation of the Napier Company in 1808. This brought the handsome Deltic 'Alycidon' of the Deltic Preservation Society onto the Buckinghamshire site.

In 2009 the opening of the site to the public reached forty years. It continues to prosper alongside the continually used Network Rail tracks passing through the centre. At the present time the line is regularly used by 2000 ton landfill rubbish trains from east and west London to the old brick pits at Calvert

Many special trains have visited the site along these metals. Notwithstanding passenger use is advancing once more north of Aylesbury to a new station at Aylesbury Parkway. It leaves the open question if it will eventually advance further?

A tank engine that had been fitted with condensing apparatus and shorter chimneys to work underground between Kings Cross and Moorgate visited Quainton in 1994. They are the LNER N2 class 0-6-2, this engine is now the only one preserved and is held at the Great Central Railway.

Andrew Bratton

A visit by LNER V2 *Green Arrow* in 2002 standing alongside platform 4. Sadly this unique locomotive has problems that may preclude it ever taking to the rails again.

Bill Simpson

On the occasion of the celebration of the Napier Engineering Company an open day was organised at Quainton with the visiting engine being the imposing preserved Napier engined Deltic 'Alycidon' from the Deltic Preservation Society.

On occasions in summer locomotives line up in steam south of the station which makes a unique photographic moment and a splendid parade of moving engines.

Bill Simpson

The situation at the end of the first decade of the 21 Century has much changed from the alarming shrinkage of the rail system of the 1960's. Closure began here with the closure of the Brill Branch and the line to Verney Junction. Now the railways are in demand with better service and speedy comfort. Delay and thrombosis of the road system proves that its prospect as a panacea confirms a grand illusion. It is still better for mass transit to be provided by the railways, if they can meet the challenge.

On March 28, 2004 the problem of footway connection between the 'up' and 'down' yards was at last solved in grand style with a magnificent modern new footbridge. Lifting this into position was a mighty proposition but it was neatly bolted into position with no problems.

Lance Adlam

The GWR pannier seen from a new vantage point with Quainton village in the background.

Bill Simpson

The 'bubble car' shuttle waits for custom with the 'Quaintonian' service to Aylesbury on the August bank holiday
Bill Simpson

Splendid work by Richard Mather restoring an exhibit of 1938 and earlier tube stock in the Museum.
Bill Simpson

In the 1970's visitors enjoyed not only a vintage carriage ride but a bit of sunbathing in open trucks! An early photograph shows the train like on the opening of the Metropolitan Underground Railway when dignitories where photographed in open trucks.

Some people may have set views about restoration and museums but the truth is that to survive sites like Quainton have to appreciate the public's requirements in the 21st century. Thus the superbly restored vintage train operates on a popular open day alongside an inflated cottage building.

Bill Simpson

The Buckinghamhsire Railway Centre provides many facilities for both leisure and study. As it welcomes a considerable number of school visits a grant was acquired to extensively restore a coach to provide a classroom environment where so many things could be studied in comfort. The volunteer carpenters carrying out the work seen here are Graham Youngman and Colin Lewis.

Bill Simpson

A considerable challenge lay ahead of Ian Miller when the Passimeter was hauled out of its dark dusty confines of storage. This work he has undertaken together with assistance of Roger Morgan to bring this Westminster (1924) station ticket office to a breathtaking magnificence. The restored beauty of the original woodwork gives a good sense of period in its design.

Bill Simpson

A view from the road bridge that passes over the line north of the station in the 1930's with the Brill mixed train patiently waiting at its platform with the A class no 23 at its head. The coach being one of the straight sided Brown-Marshall built coaches frior the Metropolitan. Note the Metropolitan signalbox in the 'down' yard that was demolished as the Quainton Railway Society were trying to raise enough money to purchase the 'up' yard.

An Interesting assembly at Quianton c1900 during Oxford & Aylesbury Tramway days. One of the Manning Wardle engines was named 'Brill No 1', the other 'Wotton'. The train is composed of a Metropolitan Railway coach with Midland Railwayfive plank wagons.

Leicestershire County Council

The Brill Branch

Anyone visiting the Buckinghamshire Railway Centre from the A41 direction will pass along the road to Quainton village probably unaware, and with some disbelief, that they are passing alongside a railway trackbed. For that entire length of road was once traversed by a railway from Quainton Road to the remote village of Brill.

The Marquess of Chandos, Duke of Buckingham, (Grenville-Temple) lived in a large country house at Wotton Underwood. The span of his estate reached almost as far as Quainton and included the village of Brill. The Duke was a keen railway promoter and enthusiast. He eventually became chairman of the mighty London & North Western Railway and once acted as fireman on an engine on the Union Pacific Railway. This made him easily convinced of the advantages of laying in some form of railway to serve the estate.

In thinking of country roads in the nineteenth century we should forget the smooth tarmacadam and well drained roads of present times, for many roads were difficult, if not impassable in the worst of the winter months. Dusty and badly rutted in summer deeply muddied and wet for many months in winter.

The estate had many extensive farming interests with milk and cereal, also with important works of local brick and tile manufacture at Wotton and Brill. Apart from the duke's enthusiasm there would be much to gain by having a light railway to serve the estate. What made it a feasible prospect was the building and opening of a new line of railway built by the Aylesbury & Buckingham Railway from Aylesbury to join the existing Oxford and Bletchley line at Claydon. For this a station was opened for the village of Quainton.

The first of the many crossings leaving Quainton where number 41 crosses over with one of the early Metropolitan coaches c1930, with a train of the usual composition. The buildings in the background remain to this day as part of a furniture making factory.

Further, the Tramways Act of August 1871 whereby the Board of Trade could sanction light railways covering certain conditions; a maximum load of 8 tons per axle, locomotive or vehicle. Also a speed limit of 12 mph. It appears also that platforms would not be required in the terms of the normal standard gauge lines. Thus the Duke could build his own light railway. The line did not require parliamentary approval by an Act as it was built almost entirely across his own land as a private railway. A short section was needed for access over land belonging to the Winwood Charity Trust with whom he was able to conclude a satisfactory agreement.

As the harvest was concluded and labour was released construction began on September 8, 1870. Twenty men were employed on pay of eleven shillings (55p) per week. It was laid with light bridge pattern rail under the organisation of Lawford & Houghton with rails rolled by Townend & Wood of Briton Ferry, South Wales. These weighed only 30 lbs per yard which compared to normal bull head rail of 75lb per yard gives an indication of their lightness.

A pathway was cleared for the line with little in the way of costly earthworks which proved a bane to later developments as the unevenness in places caused severe speed limits with very rough riding. The line was constructed with ancillary buildings influenced more by farm structures rather than railway design with platforms, such as they were, being built of earth sods with planks laid on top. The connection at Quainton was done laboriously via a wagon turntable (see ground plans).

In 2007 the original Wotton Tramway, engine, the Aveling Porter, returned to the place of the beginning of its working life. It was brought from the London Transport Museum at Covent Garden to be displayed heading a representative train from its days on the Tramway. It is seen here before entering the museum. Note the chain drive that made such a distinctive noise in the quiet fields that the locals used to say - 'ol' chaineys comin' .

Ian Miller

The terminus close to Wotton House was reached in March 1871 and to celebrate the occasion the duke distributed free coals to the community from the first operational train. The Wotton Tramway line was stipulated to be operated by horse drawn wagons which proved too restricting, the horses slipped badly in the wet and had trouble making progress.

To reach the brick works at Brill the line had to be extended beyond Wotton to the foot of the hill-top village. This allowed for a siding into the brick works. Continuing a little further a station was built alongside the Brill to Ludgershall road. This was opened for business in March 1872. and provided a valuable impetus to the burgeoning dairy production in the area.

Soon after the opening two things followed in succession. First the Duke received a request for passengers to be accommodated on the line. so that they may visit Aylesbury market. At first the Duke refused and what followed was one of the earliest examples of an industrial dispute. What leverage the locals were able to apply is not clear but many would be working on his estate either on farms or at the brickworks at Wotton and Brill. Reluctantly the Duke conceded and acquired for the service a horse drawn vehicle with two passenger compartments with a centre baggage compartment so that estate produce could be carried. A replica of this vehicle stands in the museum at Quainton behind the Wotton Tramway engine.

On December 13, 2006 the Wotton Tramway engine is taken to the Museum building needing to cross over the former Metropolitan & Great Central Joint line at Quainton on a low loader.

Ian Miller

The demands on the poor horses were alleviated by the introduction of two hybrid locomotives that were conversions of the Aveling, Porter road roller design converted to become a railway locomotive. The tramway began with a motley collection of cast off rolling stock to which the duke added the new fixed wheelbase passenger coach. Given the information of Metropolitan drivers that operated the line in its latter years, having to hang onto something in places with the roughness of the permanent way, the riding in the Ashbury carriage must have been an experience that was to be suffered, let alone one for which a person would pay for!

In 1873 the branch produced its own branch to a small brick and tile works at Kingswood moving off from behind the Wotton Underwood Church and passing alongside Yeat Farm.

In 1882 it was decided by the duke along with Sir Harry Verney, MP, Baron Ferdinand Rothschild, MP and Sir Edward Watkin that the line could gain great advantage from being extended to Oxford and so they promoted a company called-The Oxford & Aylesbury Railway which drew up plans to extend to Oxford and have a station in St Clements.

The original Wotton Tramway was absorbed by this company and the track was relaid with heavier bridge rail and two second hand 0-6-0 Manning Wardle locomotives were purchased. But the planned extension was never realised as sufficient capital could not be generated. The fact that a tunnel would have to be built to pierce the rising ground around Brill was a very negative factor. Later a less ambitious proposal for a railway of tramway regulation also failed.

The final day train at Quainton hauled by a class no 41. The last day train being made prominent by having two-coaches.

The branch continued with its curious unresolved name as its promoters faded. The duke died in March 26, 1889, Sir Harry Verney in 1894, and Baron Rothschild 1898, Sir Edward Watkin, chairman of the Metropolitan Railway in 1901. Railway companys had learned to their cost that the worst kind of undertaking to cripple any scheme was a tunnel, they were expensive and dangerous to build with continuous maintenance problems. It may have been if the Metropolitan had not been so embroiled in works with the construction of the Great Central Railway they may have considered supporting the scheme. It raises some interesting might-have-beens. The terminus in St Clements, Oxford would have had shorter mileage to London than its rivals. Later electrification of London Transport that stopped at Amersham may have been tempted to continue to Oxford with fast electrics of sub-surface stock outstripping times of the GWR and LMS.

For its continuing operation the branch did gain some positive advantages with better locomotives with which 12 mph was definitely exceeded, also two bogie coaches by the Bristol Carriage & Wagon Co. which would be marginally more comfortable than the fixed wheelbase stock. And probably be more inclined to remain on the track.

With its extension northwards Metropolitan Railway bought the parlous A&BR in 1894 and took over the running of the O&AT, though the railway remained with the company. They continued using the Manning Wardle locos for a time but with wear and tear they decided to replace them and improve the track. They re-engineered parts and utilised bull head rail defunct from another part of their system replacing the bridge rail. This enabled them to introduce heavier locomotives and coaches with an increase of the speed limit to 25 mph.

Newly turned out in its LT livery.engine No 23 was always closely associated with the line and it was rightly preserved in the LT Collection. It is seen here at Quianton Road on June 22, 1935.

First of all they ran a new tank engine 2-4-0 'D' class that had been intended for use north of Aylesbury but they proved to heavy for the branch. The Metropolitan had an extensive steam locomotive fleet of Beyer-Peacock class 'A' class 4-4-0T that had worked in the tunnels of the sub-surface underground railway. Many were displaced by electrification. These locos had a flexible wheel base which they would need for the curve at Wotton station which would have been a severe test of anything with a long wheelbase. Interestingly they were in fact older than the first locomotive used, the Aveling, Porter!

Things continued with the Metropolitan replacing the track and running the 'A' class engines with Metropolitan coaches throughout the early period of the twentieth century. The first World War came and went on its tragic course and no doubt Quainton Road served as part of the essential transport role in that period. Great Central Railway expresses to and from the north passed through platforms 1 and 2 of the newly rebuilt Quainton Road station of 1895-6. In between them the branch line style train went on its daily journeys between Aylesbury and Verney Junction calling at Grandborough Road and Winslow Road stations.

This increasingly became the type of service on that line after the first world war. The Pullman service operating from Aylesbury only. The hopes and rumours of the Brill line ever being continued to Oxford now became no more than legend.

Such a confident and composed age when the reliable use of the Bradshaw Guide could be invested in was now to become a fading glory. The forces of change are always approaching. What cannot be imagined are those caused by major wars. After the first

During steam days at Quainton the rides train moves beyond the Brill platform towards the engineering sheds giving an impression, for some passengers, of how a departing tramway train would have been experienced.

Bill Simpson

It is a remarkable fact that the first mile of the Tramway from Quainton ran alongside the road to the village. With the passing years the area has became overgrown but a pathway remains for walkers.

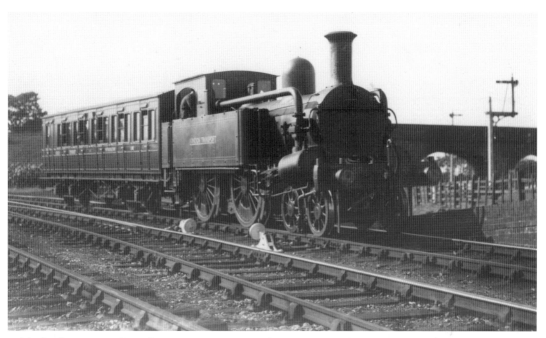

With the formation of London Transport in 1933 the name was added to the 'A' class tank engines that worked the Brill line. For only two years it was possible to see these bright red engines passing through the leafy enclosures of this attractively situated railway. Here no 23 is entering Quainton from Brill with the usual single coach.

it was the end of the former proud separate railway companies that had to amalgamate into a grouping of four. Amalgamations were the order of the time as plans were drawn up for the London transport system to be coalesced into a unified body with buses, trams and railways coming under the administration of a London Passenger Transport Board (1933). This august body decided that continuing electrification was the answer. However, it did not manage to extend from Rickmansworth to Amersham until 1960. It would have been interesting to know what might have happened if the 1882 railway to Oxford had been built.

Consequently the lines north of Amersham, including the Brill line, were left to the London & North Eastern Railway that had inherited the interests of the Great Central Railway on the Metropolitan & Great Central Joint Committee. from the grouping in 1923.

An important development where the Brill line was concerned was that lorries began picking up milk from farms in the district and delivering it to local factories like the one at Buckingham or to the special wagons in set trains at Aylesbury. By 1935 there were 435,000 motor goods vehicles registered. The railway companies themselves employed 7,650 road vehicles.

It did not take long for the LNER to serve notice of closure of the passenger services on the line to Verney Junction and for the LPTB the Brill line, total closure. This came on November 30, 1935 with a packed two coach train.

The track was soon lifted and the railway that had rattled along through wood and field was largely forgotten.

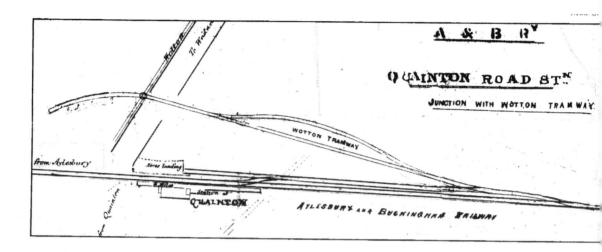

The original connection of the Wotton Tramway to the Aylesbury & Buckingham Railway at Quainton Road.

Its rotting timber buildings stood in splendid silent isolation amongst all the over-grown fertility of tree arcaded clearings of no greater noise than birdsong. Eventually they were removed to alternative use or simply crumbled to the earth. The platforms, being solid earth, remained as curious mounds for years. The houses that accommodated the staff that worked the line remained as robust habitations marking out the route of the line and can still be identified as they carry the coat of arms of the late Earl Temple, heir to the estate.

On looking at photographs and reading about this quite famous little line it is not difficult to visualise it with a kind of rustic enchantment. It brings to mind the poems reflecting the age of Hardy and Houseman. Even the locomotive engine shed for Audry's *Toby the Tram Engine* bears a remarkable resemblance to the one at Brill. It had been a useful route of transportation, probably more for goods than passenger journeys, and no doubt invoking a few curses from operators and users alike, especially when the Aveling, Porter under certain loads was inclined to leap its leading wheels from the track! But taking the broader view it was an England of few motor cars and of aeroplanes, none at all when it opened. A countryside that would have few sounds beyond birdsong and cattle noise, with horse drawn agricultural machinery in fields alongside the lumbering steam locomotive; an England difficult to imagine now.

The heroic work undertaken in the 1960's to save Quainton Road station ensured also that the memory of the Brill Branch is retained as part of the heritage of the site.

The last day on the Brill Branch

by D J McCulloch

I was fortunate enough to travel on the whole of the branch on that historic day - Saturday, November 30, 1935.

When I arrived at Quainton Road station in time for the 4.04 pm train to Brill the branch line platform presented a lovely scene with crowds of sight seers and railway officials hurrying to and fro. The platform had probably not seen so many people together on it for many years. The train consisted of Metropolitan 4-4-0T No 41, built in 1870 and two ex inner circle coaches numbered 41 and 45 of 1879. On ordinary days the train consists of one coach only but on this day the spare one, always kept at Quainton Road station, was needed. These coaches had electric lighting and one was distinguished as originally first class by the fine upholstery, the other in standard Metropolitan red and black rep. Collectively they are now considered third class as no first class accommodation was provided on the branch.

We started from Quainton Road ten minutes late (must have been getting quite dark) and only one minute later we had to stop to allow the guard to open the gates of the first crossing from the station. Having completed this and proceeded we stopped a little further on for no apparent reason.

Some three minutes later we pulled up at the first station of Waddesdon Road. This in common with all the other stations on the branch consists of a very short platform and a small hut used as a booking office and waiting room.

The remaining journey to Brill consisted largely of stopping for the level crossings and stations. We stopped for three or four minutes at each station which presented a lively scene of many people, such a distinct comparison to recent years of emptiness. If one were ignorant of the circumstances one would wonder why such a busy line would be closed down!

At Wotton we passed the disused Oxford & Aylesbury Tramroad water tank on the junction of the mile and a half branch to Kingswood running in a north-westerly direction, including Church Siding.

The LNER line to Wycombe passed over the tramroad at Wotton and formed the only overbridge on the line.

The station after Wotton was Wood Siding, near here was the short branch siding to the Brill Brickworks Co. The GWR main line of 1910 passes under the branch and part of the platform at Wood Siding which is actually on the bridge.

Just under a mile further on was Brill station and the terminus of the branch. Here there were many things of interest including an old Oxford & Aylesbury Tramroad coach consisting of three compartments the seats of which were just planks. By now it had been taken from its wheels and was a platelayers hut.

On arrival of the train at Brill most of the passengers scattered over the various sheds and sidings while others huddled around the warm fire in the small waiting room or crowded into the cab of the engine where they bombarded the driver and fireman with many questions. Of all the people there only half a dozen were regular travellers on the line. The tiny booking office was crowded with people clamouring for relics that may be left over. But apart from a few tickets there was nothing to be had.

The hour that we had to wait for the train to return passed very quickly and was of great interest. Eventually we piled into the train once more including the guards van and prepared for the return journey. I myself was lucky enough to persuade the driver to take me on the footplate; this was my first footplate run. When we had gone about half way we were startled by three loud reports and flashes from the front of the engine caused by someone placing some fireworks on the line.

As soon as we reached Quainton Road I went into the booking office to see if I could obtain some tickets or old timetables. But the only things of interest were an old issue of tickets that were still in use between Quainton Road and Waddesdon Road still marked with the initial 'O & A T' (Oxford & Aylesbury Tramroad) and also the name Waddesdon instead of Waddesdon Road, that being the old name of the station.

A few minutes later I caught my London train bringing my evening of farewell to the Brill branch to an end.

Engine no 23 arriving at Waddesdon road station. The single siding was normally occupied with local coal merchants wagons as seen here. The view is looking back towards Quainton Road.

Waddesdon Road

Incredible though it now seems that the railway station of Waddesdon Road, which was the first one from the village, was situated in the space that now exists in the corner of the junction of the village road and its joining of the A41 Bicester - Aylesbury Road. The farmhouse remains on the other side of the road where the Tramway continued with an odd wall angle caused by the line of the railway.

The station set the pattern for the stations along the line with a simple hut which served as ticket office and waiting room together with another hut to store goods requirements. The main concern besides coal and small goods was the daily collection of milk churns along the line and their subsequent return.

In calm sunshine a lone passenger waits at Waddesdon Road. The position of the station can be ascertained from the the house which still exists at the present day

One of the station posters is advertising 'Summer Tickets a penny a mile, any train any day'. A reflection of the days when a journey from this station to London would cost thirty-eight pennies! The smaller hut is likely to be original, corrugation was used on the first buildings.

Quite a contrast for the A41 road where the line crossed over compared to the busy use of it nowadays.

The view at Westcott looking towards Wotton. the platforms were rebuilt to a standard height with the introduction of more conventional coaching stock during the O&AT period.

RAS Marketing

Westcott

Unlike Waddesdon the station at Westcott was situated close alongside the village street where a pair of cottages of the Buckingham & Chandos estate were built. These would house estate employees one of which would be responsible for the maintenance and working of the Tramway business. With coal deliveries, milk collection, farm provender and a few passengers.

An A class tank entering Westcott in the early 1930's.

Bill Simpson Collection

The view of Westcott station in the early 1930's. The house was built by the Duke of Buckingham for estate staff, here for the manning of the station. Entrance to the goods and coal yard is on the left with the good shed alongside. The crossing gate is on the right.

London Transport

A very rare photograph of a 'D' class on the Brill line hauling one of the Bristol Carriage & Wagon Company coaches. Judging by the curve it would suggest just after Wotton going towards Brill.

QRS Collection

Days of summer and the ambling branch train pulling into Wotton station. No 41 makes its call in progress to Brill in the early 1930's

Wotton

Close by Wotton House, the home of the Duke of Buckingham, this station was situated on a severe curve. The arrival of a second station of the Great Central & Great Western Joint close by linked Princes Risborough with Grendon Underwood, it was opened on April 2, 1906. The bridge of this line passing over the tramway. It seems extraordinary that a place so remote and of small population should have had two stations for nearly thirty years.

Entrance to Wotton station.

Wotton station looking towards Brill with the highly individual designed goods shed on the left.
London Transport

Wotton was the most important station en route to Brill. Originally in the Duke's plan this was the end of the line until he decided to extend it to Brill. The station was used a great deal with the introduction of the GWR&GCRJoint line between Ashendon Junction and Grendon Underwood the bridge for which can be seen on the left.

An impressive view looking towards Wood Siding on the approach from Quainton. So characteristic of the area are the magnificent trees, many being oaks, suggesting the ancient forest. For many years they resounded to the echoes of passing of trains.

London Transport

Wood Siding

Amongst the peculiarities of the Brill branch, the minor status of it stations, one Halt stands out as an even greater oddity - Wood Siding. Situated alongside a wood that is reputed as a remaining fragment of the ancient Bernewood Forest, which became part of the Wotton estate. Here one porter/crossing keeper was employed in his lonely occupation, or sylvan retreat, depending on which way that one looked at it. It is doubtful that he booked many passenger journeys arriving or departing but certainly it was used as a milk collection point and coal siding.

During 1908-10 period its somnolence was greatly disturbed by the arrival of a new railway built by the GWR. This was an extended line from Princes Risborough to Aynho Junction, to join the older Oxford line. This brought the fine GWR trains passing beneath hauled by the elegant locomotives of William Dean and Churchward culminating in the toure de force of the 'Castles' and 'Kings'. Thus the vivid presentation of Brunswick Green compared to the dark red Metropolitan which changed to bright red of London Transport from 1933. Visually it could not have failed to have been an exciting scene in such a remote place.

After closure of the Tramway in 1935 the GWR opened a new Halt on their line close by on June 21, 1937 Dorton Halt; this closed on January 7, 1963.

Engine no 41 at the platform before departing for Brill. A porter that spent many years of his working life at Wood Siding was called Benny Wichert. He had a ladder fixed to the overshadowing oak tree and when a train was due to leave Brill he would climb up to see the exhaust of the climbing engine as it took the curving gradient out of Brill station. That was his cue to prepare for the arrival at Wood Siding.

Roy Slaymaker Collection

Wood Siding in the 1930's, the plate girder bridge on the left clearly shows where the GWR excavated beneath with a railway that remains intensively used by Chiltern Railways to this day.

RAS

Fine summer days at Brill station with no 41 preparing to return to Quainton with a typical branch assembly.

Brill

On its heights Brill seemed unassailable by railways until the Wotton Tramway was built to arrive on the road between Brill and Ludgershall. The hill where the characteristic windmill stands was gouged out in a number of areas where the clay had been worked to supply the local brickworks served by the tramway. The fired clay created beautiful shades of terracotta particularly attractive after summer rain. These shades give the village a pleasing warmth of colours often discovered by painters.

From the hill Wotton House can be seen amid the verdant expanse of the Vale of Aylesbury. How pleasing it must have looked to see the steam pennant winding its way towards the village. More so if one was planning to go to the station to catch the train to depart.

Although the station was some distance away it was very much a part of the village and local people gained employment on the railway or served the community as carriers.

It served in a re-invigorated way the needs of a local Farmer called Fenemore who manufactured mechanical hayloaders and used the former Brill Brickworks factory that had become redundant when brick manufacturing became concentrated in large plants of the Fletton process. So those locals made redundant found employment in the new industry. Many of the machines were transported on flat trucks along the line.

Brill station platform view with a train just arrived.

Just under half a mile from Brill station was the siding leading off to the Brill brickworks. The works became unproftable due to the expansion of the Fletton process used by the London Brick Company. Fenemore then used the siding to send out his hayloader machines.

London Transport

One of the ex-contractor Manning Wardle locomotives of the Oxford & Aylesbury Railway operating the line with straight sided Metropolitan coach. Unlike most railway employment, where staff were expected to move about the company's system the Tramway staff all came from the locality and largely speaking remained on the line. With the introduction of the A class tanks the line came into the Neasden links for footplate men.

After closure in 1935 the track was quickly removed and the buildings demolished. Leaving the land to be reclaimed as pasture. A few mounds of earth bear evidence that the line had existed. On to the right the cottages where employees lived have remained to the present day. The two original cottages were added to by a third in 1885.

The locomotive steam shed at Brill was little used in latter years when the A class engines returned to Aylesbury every evening. The building on the extreme left was the original steam shed that held the Aveling Porter locomotives.

No 23 takes much needed water at the Brill steam shed. Note the dilapidated old forge on the left. Built in the beautiful bricks and tiles of the locality it would be a good example of the artistic definition of 'pleasing in decay'.

Not a very clear print as it is taken from an old Railway Magazine but it is useful to include as it shows the two Bristol Carriage Co coaches at Brill and the coach built by the duke also. Barely visible is the light tramway track of the original Wotton Tramway which gives some indication of the look of the original railway.

The train at Brill on a fine day waiting to depart back to Quainton. This would be in the latter days as it has the London Transport logo type style on the side.

Brill station probably early in the twentieth century showing one of the Manning Wardle locomotives with the Metropolitan 'MR' on the buffer beam. Note the round topped door on the vintage carriage, distinctive to underground stock.

QRS Collection